MASTERING COBOL: A COMPREHENSIVE GUIDE TO MODERN PROGRAMMING IN COBOL

DR ASHOK JAHAGIRDAR | PHD
(INFPRRNATION TECHNOLOGY)

Copyright © Dr Ashok Jahagirdar, PhD (Infprrnation
Technology)
All Rights Reserved.

This book has been self-published with all reasonable efforts taken
to make the material error-free by the author. No part of this
book shall be used, reproduced in any manner whatsoever without
written permission from the author, except in the case of brief
quotations embodied in critical articles and reviews.

The Author of this book is solely responsible and liable for its
content including but not limited to the views, representations,
descriptions, statements, information, opinions and references
["Content"]. The Content of this book shall not constitute or be
construed or deemed to reflect the opinion or expression of the
Publisher or Editor. Neither the Publisher nor Editor endorse or
approve the Content of this book or guarantee the reliability,
accuracy or completeness of the Content published herein and do
not make any representations or warranties of any kind, express
or implied, including but not limited to the implied warranties of
merchantability, fitness for a particular purpose. The Publisher and
Editor shall not be liable whatsoever for any errors, omissions,
whether such errors or omissions result from negligence, accident,
or any other cause or claims for loss or damages of any kind,
including without limitation, indirect or consequential loss or
damage arising out of use, inability to use, or about the reliability,
accuracy or sufficiency of the information contained in this book.

Made with ♥ on the Notion Press Platform
www.notionpress.com

Contents

Preface

Dear Reader,

It gives me immense pleasure to introduce this book, an ode to a programming language that has been the cornerstone of my journey and the starting point of my career—COBOL. As I reminisce about my initial days as a COBOL Programmer on the ICL 2904/50 mainframe, it fills me with nostalgia and gratitude for the foundation it provided me in the realm of programming.

While my roots were firmly planted in COBOL, my curiosity and eagerness to explore led me down diverse paths. Today, I find myself not just delving into COBOL intricacies but also traversing the landscapes of C++, Java, and Python, teaching and guiding eager minds through the intricacies of these powerful programming languages.

Moreover, my journey expanded beyond conventional classrooms. I realized the critical importance of empowering corporate executives with fundamental computer skills to thrive in today's digital era. Witnessing their empowerment and newfound confidence in the realm of technology has been immensely rewarding.

The digital revolution knows no bounds, and neither should education. Hence, I ventured into the realm of online teaching, reaching students scattered across the four corners of the earth. This endeavor has been humbling, breaking geographical barriers and fostering a global community of learners passionate about mastering programming languages.

This book is a culmination of my experiences, expertise, and passion for COBOL programming. It aims not only to elucidate the technical nuances but also to serve as a guiding light for beginners and enthusiasts alike, offering insights garnered from my diverse journey in the tech realm.

As you embark on this journey through the pages of this book, I hope it serves as a compass, guiding you through the intricate yet fascinating world of COBOL programming. May it ignite your curiosity, expand your knowledge, and empower you to venture further into the ever-evolving universe of technology.

Warm regards,

Dr. Ashok Jahagirdar

PhD (Information Technology)

CHAPTER ONE

Working with Data in COBOL

Data Definition and Usage

COBOL's strength lies in its ability to handle various types of data used in business applications. The Data Division in COBOL is where data structures are defined, allowing programmers to work with different data elements.

DATA DESCRIPTION ENTRIES (DDTS)

COBOL uses DATA DESCRIPTION ENTRIES (DDEs) to define data elements. These entries describe the characteristics of the data items used in the program. Each DDE contains information about the data's name, length, type, and usage.

Data Types in COBOL

COBOL supports different data types:

NUMERIC:

Used for integers and decimals. Examples include PIC 9(5) for a five-digit numeric field and PIC 9(3)V99 for a three-digit whole number with a two-decimal place fractional part.

ALPHABETIC:

Represents alphanumeric data like names, addresses, etc. Examples include PIC X(20) for a 20-character string.

ALPHANUMERIC EDITED:

Allows data to be displayed with special characters or formats. For instance, PIC $9,999.99 represents a formatted monetary value.

GROUP DATA ITEMS:

Enables grouping of related data elements. It's declared using the GROUP keyword.

Data Manipulation in COBOL

Once data elements are defined, they can be manipulated using various operations:

MOVE:

Transfers data from one data item to another.

ADD, SUBTRACT, MULTIPLY, DIVIDE: Arithmetic operations performed on numeric data.

COMPUTE:

Performs arithmetic calculations involving multiple operations.

STRING:

Concatenates or combines strings of characters.

INSPECT:

Scans and manipulates data based on specified criteria.

Example: Employee Data Record

Let's consider an example of defining and using an employee data record in COBOL:

```
IDENTIFICATION DIVISION.
PROGRAM-ID. EMPLOYEE-DATA.
DATA DIVISION.
WORKING-STORAGE SECTION.
01 EMPLOYEE-RECORD.
05 EMPLOYEE-ID PIC 9(5).
05 EMPLOYEE-NAME PIC X(30).
```

```
05 EMPLOYEE-SALARY PIC 9(6)V99.
PROCEDURE DIVISION.
MAIN-PROCEDURE.
MOVE 12345 TO EMPLOYEE-ID.
MOVE "Ashok J" TO EMPLOYEE-NAME.
MOVE 5000.75 TO EMPLOYEE-SALARY.
DISPLAY "Employee ID: " EMPLOYEE-ID.
DISPLAY "Employee Name: " EMPLOYEE-NAME.
DISPLAY "Employee Salary: " EMPLOYEE-SALARY.
STOP RUN.
```

In this example, we define an employee record structure containing an ID, name, and salary. Then, we assign values to these fields and display them using the DISPLAY statement.

CHAPTER TWO

Introduction to COBOL

History and Evolution

COBOL (Common Business-Oriented Language) was developed in the late 1950s by a committee led by Grace Hopper. It was designed specifically for business data processing applications, focusing on readability, simplicity, and a high-level language approach.

The language gained popularity due to its English-like syntax, making it accessible for non-programmers to understand and maintain. Over the years, COBOL evolved through various versions, adapting to changing computing environments while maintaining backward compatibility.

Basic Structure and Syntax

COBOL programs are divided into divisions:

Identification Division,

Environment Division,

Data Division,

Procedure Division, and

Report Writer.

Each division serves a specific purpose:

Identification Division:

Contains information about the program such as name, author, date, etc.

The Identification Division in COBOL is the section where essential information about the program is specified. It typically contains the following elements:

PROGRAM-ID:

This statement identifies the name of the COBOL program. It's a mandatory statement that gives the program a unique identifier.

AUTHOR:

Specifies the name of the person who wrote the program.

INSTALLATION:

Describes the organization or company where the program was developed.

DATE-WRITTEN:

Indicates the date when the program was originally written or last modified.

DATE-COMPILED:

Shows the date when the program was compiled.

REMARKS:

Provides any additional comments or remarks about the program.

Here is an example of the Identification Division in COBOL:

IDENTIFICATION DIVISION.

PROGRAM-ID. SAMPLE-PROGRAM.

AUTHOR. Ashok J.

DATE-WRITTEN. 2023-12-23.

DATE-COMPILED. 2023-12-24.

REMARKS. This is a sample COBOL program for demonstration purposes.

The Identification Division is essential for documenting crucial details about the COBOL program, aiding in program maintenance, and providing context to anyone working on or reviewing the code.

Environment Division:

Specifies the configuration and external resources used by the program.

Data Division:

Declares data structures, defining the data elements used in the program.

Procedure Division:

Contains the actual logic and instructions to process data.

Report Writer:

Defines formatted reports if needed.

Data Types and Structures

COBOL supports various data types:

NUMERIC:

Numeric data such as integers and decimals (e.g., PIC 9(5), PIC 9(3)V99).

ALPHABETIC:

Alphanumeric data (e.g., PIC X(20)).

ALPHANUMERIC EDITED:

Formatted data with special characters (e.g., PIC $9,999.99).

GROUP DATA ITEMS:

Structures to hold related data fields (e.g., GROUP).

Hello World Example in COBOL

A traditional "Hello, World!" program in COBOL looks like this:

IDENTIFICATION DIVISION.

PROGRAM-ID. HELLO-WORLD.

PROCEDURE DIVISION.

DISPLAY "Hello, World!".

STOP RUN.

Explanation:

IDENTIFICATION DIVISION declares the program ID.

PROCEDURE DIVISION contains the logic.

DISPLAY is used to output text.

STOP RUN terminates the program.

This simple example illustrates the basic structure of a COBOL program, with minimal instructions required to display a message.

CHAPTER THREE

Programming Constructs in COBOL

Control Structures

COBOL offers various control structures that enable programmers to manage the flow of execution within their programs.

1. IF-ELSE Statements

IF condition-1

perform statement-1

ELSE

perform statement-2

END-IF.

Example:

IF EMPLOYEE-SALARY > 5000

DISPLAY "High Salary"

ELSE

DISPLAY "Low Salary"

END-IF.

2. PERFORM Statements

PERFORM varying-counter FROM 1 BY 1 UNTIL condition

perform statement

END-PERFORM.

Example:
PERFORM VARYING I FROM 1 BY 1 UNTIL I > 10
DISPLAY "Value of I: " I
END-PERFORM.
3. EVALUATE Statement
EVALUATE True-Condition
WHEN Value-1
perform statement-1
WHEN Value-2
perform statement-2
WHEN OTHER
perform default-statement
END-EVALUATE.
Example:
EVALUATE TRUE
WHEN EMPLOYEE-TYPE = 'Manager'
DISPLAY "Managerial Role"
WHEN EMPLOYEE-TYPE = 'Employee'
DISPLAY "Regular Employee"
WHEN OTHER
DISPLAY "Unknown Role"
END-EVALUATE.
PROCEDURES AND FUNCTIONS
COBOL allows programmers to encapsulate logic into procedures or functions for better modularity and code reusability.

Example of a Procedure
PROCEDURE DIVISION.
MAIN-PROCEDURE.
PERFORM CALCULATE-TOTAL.
STOP RUN.
CALCULATE-TOTAL.

```
COMPUTE   TOTAL-SALARY   =   BASIC-SALARY   +
ALLOWANCES.
DISPLAY "Total Salary: " TOTAL-SALARY.
```

CHAPTER FOUR

Advanced COBOL Programming

SUBPROGRAMS AND SUBROUTINES

COBOL supports the use of subprograms or subroutines to break down programs into smaller, manageable parts, promoting code reuse and better organization.

Example of Subroutine:

```
IDENTIFICATION DIVISION.
PROGRAM-ID. MAIN-PROGRAM.
DATA DIVISION.
WORKING-STORAGE SECTION.
01 RESULT PIC 9(4).
PROCEDURE DIVISION.
MAIN-LOGIC.
PERFORM MULTIPLY-OPERATION USING 12, 10.
DISPLAY "Result: " RESULT.
STOP RUN.
MULTIPLY-OPERATION.
ACCEPT ARGUMENT-1, ARGUMENT-2.
COMPUTE RESULT = ARGUMENT-1 * ARGUMENT-2.
```

EXCEPTION HANDLING

COBOL provides mechanisms to handle exceptional conditions during program execution, enhancing robustness.

Example of Exception Handling:
PROCEDURE DIVISION.
MAIN-LOGIC.
PERFORM DIVISION-OPERATION.
DISPLAY "Result: " RESULT.
STOP RUN.
DIVISION-OPERATION.
DIVIDE 10 BY 0 GIVING RESULT
ON SIZE ERROR
DISPLAY "Division by Zero Error"
NOT ON SIZE ERROR
DISPLAY "Division Successful"
END-DIVIDE.

DEBUGGING TECHNIQUES

Debugging in COBOL can be done through various methods:

DISPLAY Statements:

Output intermediate results to trace program flow.

COBOL Debugging Tools:

Utilize debugging tools provided by specific COBOL compilers.

Use of Inspection Statements: INSPECT statement helps in analyzing and manipulating data.

Subroutines enhance code modularity, making programs more manageable. Exception handling helps manage errors and unexpected situations gracefully.

Debugging techniques play a vital role in identifying and rectifying issues within COBOL programs.

CHAPTER FIVE

COBOL in Modern Environments

Integration with Other Languages

COBOL has adapted to work alongside modern programming languages and technologies for seamless integration within diverse computing environments.

Example of Integration:

```
PROCEDURE DIVISION.
MAIN-LOGIC.
CALL "MY_JAVA_FUNCTION" USING ARG1, ARG2.
DISPLAY "Returned from Java function".
STOP RUN.
```

Here, COBOL can invoke a Java function (MY_JAVA_FUNCTION) using a CALL statement, passing arguments and receiving results.

COBOL IN OBJECT-ORIENTED PROGRAMMING (OOP)

While originally procedural, COBOL has evolved to incorporate object-oriented concepts, allowing for the creation and usage of objects, classes, and inheritance in some implementations.

WEB DEVELOPMENT WITH COBOL

COBOL is also utilized in web development. Various frameworks and tools enable COBOL applications to interact with web services, databases, and create web-based interfaces.

Example of COBOL Web Service Integration:

```
IDENTIFICATION DIVISION.
PROGRAM-ID. WEB-SERVICE-EXAMPLE.
DATA DIVISION.
WORKING-STORAGE SECTION.
01 RESPONSE PIC X(100).
PROCEDURE DIVISION.
MAIN-LOGIC.
CALL 'REST_API_ENDPOINT' USING WS-REQUEST, WS-RESPONSE.
DISPLAY "Response from Web Service: " WS-RESPONSE.
STOP RUN.
```

This code snippet showcases a COBOL program interacting with a RESTful web service by calling its endpoint and displaying the received response.

Despite its age, COBOL remains critical in various industries, especially banking, insurance, and government sectors. Its reliability and robustness make it a preferred choice for mission-critical systems.

FUTURE PROSPECTS

While newer languages have gained popularity, COBOL continues to have a significant presence. The demand for COBOL skills remains steady, and efforts to modernize COBOL systems ensure its relevance in evolving technology landscapes

CHAPTER SIX

COBOL Best Practices Writing Clean and Readable Code

Meaningful Naming:

Use descriptive names for variables, functions, and procedures to enhance code readability.

Comments:

Include clear and concise comments to explain complex logic or sections of code.

Consistent Indentation and Formatting:

Maintain consistent indentation and formatting to improve code structure and readability.

PERFORMANCE OPTIMIZATION

Efficient Data Usage:

Optimize data definitions to use minimal memory while ensuring accuracy.

Avoiding Redundancy:

Refrain from redundant computations or unnecessary loops to improve execution speed.

Use of Indexing:

Utilize indexing for faster access to data elements in arrays or tables.

DOCUMENTATION AND MAINTENANCE

Detailed Documentation:

Provide comprehensive documentation to facilitate easier maintenance and understanding of the codebase.

Version Control:

Employ version control systems to track changes and manage code revisions effectively.Refactoring and Code Reviews: Regularly review and refactor code for better maintainability and readability.

ERROR HANDLING AND VALIDATION

Robust Error Handling:

Implement thorough error handling mechanisms to manage exceptions and unexpected scenarios.

Input Validation:

Validate user inputs rigorously to prevent errors and ensure data integrity.

Logging and Reporting:

Implement logging mechanisms to track errors and generate reports for debugging and analysis.

TESTING AND QUALITY ASSURANCE

Comprehensive Testing:

Conduct thorough testing of the COBOL application to identify and rectify bugs.

Test Automation:

Automate test cases where possible to streamline the testing process and ensure consistent results.

Code Reviews:

Conduct peer code reviews to identify potential issues and improve code quality.

Real-World Applications of COBOL

BANKING SYSTEMS

COBOL has been a cornerstone in banking and finance. It manages core functions like transaction processing, account management, and statement generation due to its reliability and robustness.

INSURANCE INDUSTRY

In the insurance sector, COBOL is extensively used for policy management, claims processing, and handling vast amounts of data efficiently.

GOVERNMENT SYSTEMS

COBOL is prevalent in government agencies for managing social security systems, tax processing, and administrative operations due to its stability and scalability.

HEALTHCARE SECTOR

Many healthcare organizations rely on COBOL for managing patient records, billing systems, and healthcare data processing due to its ability to handle large volumes of data securely.

LEGACY SYSTEMS MODERNIZATION

Despite the rise of newer technologies, many organizations continue to maintain and modernize existing

COBOL systems rather than replacing them entirely. Modernization efforts often involve integrating COBOL with newer technologies to enhance functionality and interface.

CHALLENGES AND OPPORTUNITIES

While COBOL continues to play a vital role in various industries, there are challenges such as a diminishing pool of COBOL programmers and the need for system modernization. However, these challenges also present opportunities for skilled COBOL developers and initiatives focused on system migration and modernization.

Future Trends and Advancements in COBOL

CONTINUED RELEVANCE

Despite its age, COBOL remains integral to many industries due to its stability and robustness. Its relevance persists in critical systems, and efforts to modernize COBOL applications are ongoing.

COBOL IN CLOUD COMPUTING

Adoption of COBOL in cloud environments is increasing. Cloud-native COBOL solutions are being developed, allowing COBOL applications to run in cloud infrastructures, providing scalability and flexibility.

INTEGRATION WITH MODERN TECHNOLOGIES

COBOL is being integrated with modern technologies and frameworks, enabling interoperability with newer languages, databases, and platforms, enhancing its capabilities.

AGILE AND DEVOPS PRACTICES

Adopting agile methodologies and DevOps practices in COBOL development is gaining traction, enabling faster iterations, continuous integration, and deployment, aligning COBOL with modern software development practices.

EDUCATION AND SKILL DEVELOPMENT

Efforts are underway to educate and train new developers in COBOL, ensuring a continued workforce to maintain and modernize existing systems.

AUTOMATED MODERNIZATION TOOLS

Tools and technologies are being developed for automating the modernization of COBOL systems, facilitating a smoother transition to newer platforms without rewriting the entire codebase.

The future of COBOL involves a blend of its enduring legacy and adaptation to contemporary technologies. Continued modernization efforts, integration with cloud computing, adoption of agile practices, and the evolution of development tools contribute to the sustained relevance and advancement of COBOL in the ever-changing landscape of technology. Understanding these trends is vital for leveraging COBOL's strengths while embracing the advancements shaping its future.

www.ingramcontent.com/pod-product-compliance
Lightning Source LLC
Chambersburg PA
CBHW041649150726

48005CB00015BB/2566